MARKETING TO THE
MILLENNIAL WOMAN

MARKETING

TO THE

MILLENNIAL
WOMAN

BY
ANN ARNOF FISHMAN

**GENERATIONAL
TARGETED
MARKETING**

Marketing to the Millennial Woman by Ann Arnof Fishman
Generational Targeted Marketing, LLC

www.annfishman.com

To reach the author or Generational Targeted Marketing, LLC
email: ann@annfishman.com

ISBN: 978-0-692-47239-2

Other available versions:
Digital Distribution
ISBN: 978-0-692-47240-8

Manufactured in the United States of America
First Edition

Cover design by Walker & Associates

Design and composition by John Lotte for Meryl Moss Media
merylmossmedia.com

*T*o my son John,

who, in spite of his own workload, created

my websites, negotiated my contracts,

kept me on a straight and narrow path

("You're not supposed to know it all, Mom—

don't step beyond your field of expertise."),

critiqued clients' websites, co-presented

at the NSA when I needed his expertise on

organizational skills, and, most importantly,

brings joy and laughter to my life.

And in memory of my mentor, Dorothy Sarnoff,

who believed in me.

CONTENTS

ACKNOWLEDGMENTS

Linda Cain who started me on the path to the study of America's six generations.

Retired Senator David Pryor who was willing to explore new generational concepts that moved America forward.

My clients who added their expertise of services and products to my knowledge of generations to create something new.

Jonathan Vespa, demographer at the U.S. Census Bureau, for sharing his expertise.

Babbie Lovett who encouraged me.

Elayne Snyder, editor and speech coach extraordinaire, who gave my writing clarity without losing my voice.

Stephanie J. Beavers Communications for providing editorial support.

Wonder Woman who summed up millennial women quite nicely when she said: ". . . you know who I am . . . who the world needs me to be. I'm Wonder Woman."[1]

Thanks to all of you!

WHY MILLENNIAL WOMEN MATTER!

Millennials, aka *gen Ys,* were born between 1982 and 2000. Today, they number about eighty million men and women[2] and account for a quarter of the population of the United States.

Like all generations, millennials are shaped by the historic events that occurred during their formative years. These historic events create generational characteristics that will be tempered by age and current events but will otherwise stay with a generation through its lifespan. Millennials' characteristics forever impact their values, attitudes, lifestyles, and priorities.

Forty million millennial women[3] prefer to shop at, and work for, certain types of companies. This book explains how those companies attract and retain them, and will help you capture this coveted market as well. To successfully market to millennial women you must understand what drives them, and then figure out how your products and services fit in with that lifestyle.

The author explains which methods of communication and social media the millennial woman prefers, which companies get their marketing right, and what millennial women expect from businesses.

If your product doesn't mesh with the millennial woman's lifestyle, there's no amount or type of marketing that will change that. But if there is a match, what this book will give you is a decisive marketing edge with a generation that is redefining the American woman and influencing every aspect of American business.

1

Millennials' Concerns Must Be Your Concerns

Companies that seek millennials' business are companies that promote millennial social values and concerns.

At an earlier age than previous generations, millennials demonstrated concerns about others, about the environment, and about global conditions. To capture the millennial market, their concerns must also be yours.

Concern for Others Millennial women care about others. Their lives are driven by purpose. During their formative years, they watched a media that focused on those who devoted their lives to helping people in need around the world. Millennials were affected by the deaths of Princess Diana and Mother Teresa—well-known women who devoted their lives to helping others. Millennial women want to be like them.

On TV and the Internet, millennials also witnessed their peers and idols demonstrating care for others around the world at Live 8, a day-long series of global benefit concerts that took place in July of 2005. The concerts encouraged aid in the fight against poverty, particularly in Africa. Of course benefit concerts were popular with other generations, too. But, Live 8 went global and live. That's millennial.

Unlike previous generations, millennials have been dedicated volunteers since pre-K. That caring attitude has stayed with them. They are the first generation where questions about their volunteer activity are so fundamental they often appear on college admission forms.

At Tulane University, for example, it's part of the curriculum. Tulane requires students to complete a *major volunteer project* each year in order to graduate.

Concern about the Environment Millennial women care about the environment. Companies that seek millennials' business are companies that promote environmental causes.

Environmentally friendly products win millennial approval, as do the companies that provide them. Starbucks stores, a millennial-favored meeting place, practice both energy and water conservation, provide recycling facilities, and use cups that are recyclable.

Working conditions that consider safety and the environment also factor into millennials' buying decisions. Apple created the Environment, Health, and Safety Academy which trains employees globally to identify and solve problems such as how to protect a lake near Shanghai that is used as a source of drinking water from becoming polluted due to factory water drains.[4]

Concern about Global Conditions → Millennials are drawn to companies that show understanding and support of global conditions.

As little girls, millennials played with American Girl dolls. Each doll comes with her own story and history as told through accompanying books that cover topics such as child labor, child abuse, poverty, and animal abuse. American Girl created a doll collection called "Girls of Many Lands" that highlighted historic events in each country represented.

Going global has always been a part of millennial women's lives. They have contacts around the world, some as friends, some as modern-day pen pals with whom they interact on chatboards (such as Reddit). They know what's going on in remote villages and in town squares. They use the Internet to widen their worldly knowledge and deepen their concern and commitment.

Having a global view of the world is the millennial norm. They vacation and study abroad. They shop internationally via the Internet. Younger millennial women vicariously travel the globe and absorb other cultures by watching TV series such as *The Amazing Race, The Bachelor/Bachelorette,* and *Covert Affairs.*

Millennial girls and women respond deeply to people in need around the world, and they want to work for, and shop at, companies that care.

2

The Three Words That Reveal What Millennial Women Want

1. Empowerment
2. Information
3. Groups

Empowerment!

During their childhood:

- 80% of millennials grew up with parental encouragement.[5]

- Child care was more important to voters than any other issue.[6]

- A political action committee benefitting children, KIDS-PAC, was formed in 1988 to lobby for children's interests.[7]

- Federal spending for all manner of legislation from highways to budget deficits was measured and promoted in terms of, "Is it good for the children?"

A societal support system this strong has given millennials a desire for empowerment and a feeling of entitlement.

Empowered millennials are drawn to companies that help them get ahead. As employees, millennials expect to be leaders of industry, technology, government, the arts—almost anything at the top and, reasonable or not, they expect to achieve leadership roles quickly. Because of this, millennials drive employers crazy.

Marketers, however, can make this desire for empowerment work in their favor by helping millennial women achieve the success they feel they deserve.

Companies are responding. The cosmetic company L'Oréal supports girls in the area of science. From their website: "We can interest more young people in science—especially girls—if, along with equations, calculations and chemical reactions, we also show them how science helps people and how important it is to solving the world's problems."[8]

Millennials feel empowered and want to make a grand statement in their lives.

Information!

Millennial women have a strong, almost compulsive need to share information.

Millennials are the first generation to grow up in a digital world. Sharing information is considered a survival skill to them, and social networks help them tell it all.

The most popular social networking sites as of June 2014 were, in order: Facebook, Twitter, LinkedIn, Pinterest, Google+, Tumblr, Instagram, VKontakte, Flickr, and Myspace.[9]

How can you take advantage of social networking sites to promote your products or services?

To keep current, check out business magazine *Fast Company*'s yearly list of the top ten most innovative companies in social media. In 2014, the magazine highlighted **Twitter** for its brevity and video, **WhatsApp** for attracting the under-twenty-fives who are less in love with Facebook, **Snapchat** for helping people manage the overabundance of media, **Tinder** for putting the fun back into dating, and **Whisper** for offering a secret place to communicate in a public world.[10]

Keeping current is the key. Connecting to the right social medium is important for businesses. Knowing what captivates the millennial audience for your products and services is an ongoing challenge. What's hot now won't necessarily be hot in a year or two.

Forbes also alerts readers to social media companies that are worth following. Some mentioned in 2014 were: @TEDTalks (twitter.com/TEDTalks) for its variety of expert speakers, Old Spice (youtube.com/user/OldSpice/videos) for making viral videos that rock, @eat24 (https://twitter.com/eat24) for appealing to foodies, @Charmin (twitter.com/Charmin) for its inappropriate #tweetsfromtheseat, @XBoxSupport (twitter.com/XboxSupport) for its rapid response to customers with problems, T-Mobile USA (facebook.com/TMobile) for answering 86% of questions asked, and Oscar de la Renta (instagram.com/oscarprgirl) for giving a sneak peek at fashions to come.[11]

Designating someone within your company (perhaps a knowledgeable millennial) to keep on top of which social media your customers are reacting to is a good idea.

It is not enough for a company to merely have a social presence; the important thing is to have a unique and engaging presence. *Forbes.com* contributor Kate Taylor has a good sense for what makes a website stand out. Here are some she mentioned in 2013: [12]

- Rookie   www.rookiemag.com
- Her Campus   www.hercampus.com
- 20-Nothings   www.20-nothings.com
- Career Sushi   www.careersushi.com
- Ed2010   www.ed2010.com
- Girls Who Code   www.girlswhocode.com
- Her Agenda   www.heragenda.com
- Generation Meh   www.generationmeh.com
- Quarterlette   www.quarterlette.com
- HelloGiggles   www.hellogiggles.com

These sites are a part of millennial women's conversations because they address topics millennials want to discuss. **Quarterlette** covers whatever keeps millennial women up at night, from switching careers to dating apps. **Career Sushi** showcases talent and helps ambitious millennials find careers as well as switch jobs. (This generation switches jobs quite often if they are bored or perceive they are not moving ahead quickly enough.)

Once you connect with millennial women, they will do your marketing outreach for you by speaking with their friends about your products and services.

Millennials are the social generation. They are their own press agents and they want to be yours—on Facebook, YouTube, Twitter, Instagram, etc. And, they're good at it. They research products and services on Amazon, in chatrooms, on blogs, and from friends. Then, and only then, do they decide what the best purchase is.

A good example is Jessica, a sixteen-year-old California junior who worked summers cleaning houses to save enough to put a down payment on her first car. Typical of her generation, she did her own research (online), and finally decided on the Honda Civic.

When Jessica went to the Honda dealer, she was ignored. So she went to a Nissan dealer and ended up with a Nissan Sentra. Jessica so appreciated the salesperson's attitude as well as the car that she used word-of-mouth marketing—a strong motivator among millennials—and convinced her best friend to buy a Nissan, too.

When word-of-mouth marketing takes hold, word spreads so fast it's viral. Swiffer disposable cleaning cloths have always been a millennial favorite. Proctor & Gamble did not actively market Swiffer to millennials, but millennials told each other about the product.

Groups!

If one millennial has a good experience with a product or service, all her friends will know about it because they are a generation of groups, not individuals. This generation was team-taught and team-graded. They were awarded for simply showing up for team sports.

An east coast college sorority wanted a sorority perfume. They voted on it and went as a group to the mall, and every one of them purchased the group-favored scent. That's millennial group-think!

Thomson Safaris, a Massachusetts-based travel agency that specializes in tours to Africa, hired a generational marketing specialist to speak to their well-traveled employees about generational attitudes. Employees were asked to submit their favorite photos, and every photo sent in by a millennial employee featured a group—a group of people, a group of animals, or a mix of animals and people. Always a group.

Group thinking can work both ways. Millennials start it and marketers profit from it! Group discounts are an easy way to attract millennial customers. For example, when a millennial shops and brings one friend along, each friend receives a 10% discount off their purchase. When she brings two friends, each gets 20% off. When she brings three friends, they all get 30% off. You'll have to set the cap.

The three words that reveal what millennial women want most are empowerment, information, and groups!

3

What Tailoring, ♡Tattooing, and Technology Have to Do with Marketing

Millennials expect businesses to understand their style and their lifestyle.

The fashion-conscious millennial woman believes the right look empowers her, regardless of her size or shape.

Millennial women are fashionistas. TV shows and movies respond to her appetite for fashion. Everything is clothes, clothes, clothes.

Project Runway (Bravo) follows the process of clothing design and creation. *Dance Moms* (Lifetime) highlights the rigors and glamour of dancing, as does *Dancing with the Stars* (ABC). *Kim of Queens* (Lifetime) presented an insider's view to the world of beauty pageants. *Drop Dead Diva* (Lifetime) featured a well-dressed, sexy, plus-size heroine. *Sex and the City* (HBO), in spite of the show's title, is all about clothes. And, the main character in *The Hunger Games* trilogy, Katniss Everdeen, is described by another character as "the best dressed rebel in history."

Pervasive throughout millennials' lives is an emphasis on fashion. Dressing up Barbie and American Girl dolls taught them styling. The doll beauty salon inside its Manhattan American Girl store is a favorite outing. Listening to their brand-conscious baby boomer mothers and grandmothers talk labels has made millennials equally brand-conscious.

QVC, the television home shopping channel, teaches millennials everything they need to know about precious gems, clothing construction, make-up, and hair care.

Online shopping sites showcase global trends in women's clothes. Fashion blogs teach millennials how to create high fashion for less, and how to purchase Gucci, Louis Vuitton, Prada, and other high-end designers online at consignment websites, and offline at outlet malls, consignment shops, and store sales.

Millennial women respond to fashion marketing. The social intelligence company NetBase Solutions, Inc. commissioned Edison Research to survey a representative sample of American women aged eighteen to twenty-four regarding what influences their purchases. They surveyed over one thousand female social media users in May 2013[13] and identified several trends:

- 63% look to fashion blogs and message boards for style and trends.

- 58% look to Pinterest for accessories, special occasion clothing, and casual clothing.

- 54% look to Facebook for casual clothing and accessories, even if it's just looking at friends' photos to see what they're wearing.

- 49% look to Instagram for accessories, casual clothing, cosmetics, and special occasion footwear.

A major influence on millennial women's style and lifestyle is their need for customization and personalization.

If you've ever wondered about tattoos on young people, it's a matter of personalization, as are body piercings and brightly dyed hair. From their ring tones and case covers for their mobile phones to the patterns on their polished fingernails, millennial women love personalization.

Toyota builds a car aimed at millennials: the Scion. When the Scion first came out in 2002, it was unusual in that the number of options offered allowed millennial drivers to design their own version of the car. Today, many carmakers offer customization simply because they know millennials want it.

Small businesses can also appeal to millennials' need for personalization. A small-town florist, for a fee, invites millennials in the day before Mother's Day for a workshop on how to create personalized floral arrangements for mom. The fee for the event goes to charity. What could be more millennial!

Another example of how companies recognize millennials' need for personalization is apparent in a *Wall Street Journal* article about blue jeans trends.[14] The article talks about all the options people have when they pick out a pair of jeans: straight leg, boot cut, skinny, with zippers, buttons, extra pockets, sanded, distressed, plain, blue, another color, etc.

Technology greatly impacted the millennial woman's formative years. She doesn't know life without the Internet, text messaging, and instant messaging. She is used to responding to contests, reality TV eliminations, and opinion polls.

As a result, the millennial woman expects an interactive, hands-on approach from businesses. She wants you to market *with* her, not *to* her. She craves this hands-on connection and wants to be part of your marketing campaigns and product development.

The Build-A-Bear company understands millennials' hands-on mentality. They invite young customers to customize bears and other stuffed animals. But millennials do more than choose the animal; they customize its clothing, style, nationality, stuffing, scent, accessories, and even dialogue.

The TV industry invites millennials to express their opinions. *Glee* (FOX) hashtags #glee. *The Voice* (NBC) goes interactive by placing its Twitter handle (#TheVoice) on-screen during the show so viewers can vote to save contestants from elimination. On *Bones* (FOX), fans and followers can download the music played during the programs and tweet questions about the show to the actors during live Twitter sessions. While all shows now have a social-networking presence, some are more active and effective at it.

Businesses of any size profit from marketing to millennials on Facebook. When a user *likes* a company's Facebook page, the company then shows up under the user's interests and becomes instantly visible to potentially countless other Facebook users in the process. Companies act on this presence by offering those who have liked their page special access to coupons and merchandise.

Susquehanna University (Selinsgrove, PA) president Jay Lemons invites students to dine with him at some point during their college career. Invitations come with a discussion agenda: why they chose Susquehanna, what they enjoy most, and what they would change if they were president.

Marketers watch millennial consumers, looking for trends and preferences. What's new and unique is that millennial women watch back and raise the bar on interaction.

Millennial women want businesses to understand their love of fashion, their need for personalization, and their desire for interaction.

4

Millennial Women's Primary Influencers Are Both Real and Fictional

To sell to this generation of women, it pays to know the role models who have significantly impacted millennial shopping behavior.

These role models are the women who have influenced their values, attitudes, and priorities.

Millennials adored Princess Diana. Although she died in 1997 at the age of thirty-six, Diana made her place in history as a humanitarian, as a passionate champion of the rights of the disadvantaged, and as an advocate for people with AIDS.

Mother Teresa, the Roman Catholic sister, lived most of her life in India. Her mission to help others has deeply affected millennial women. The media coverage following her death—also in 1997—was worldwide.

During 1997 and 1998, television screens were filled with images of Princess Diana and Mother Teresa—two very different women. Millennial women were drawn to them, and so it follows, millennial women are drawn to companies who support causes they perceive as important. Millennial women prefer to shop at, and work for, companies who support people in need.

Women who excel in real life become instant role models to millennial women. Dara Torres, twelve-time Olympic medalist, is one such woman. Tommie Copper, a company that specializes in enhanced performance exercise apparel, featured Torres in one of their TV commercials.

Sheryl Sandberg, Facebook's Chief Operating Officer and author of the best seller *Lean In*, encourages young women to become role models themselves. *Lean In for Graduates* is Sandberg's follow-up book targeted especially to millennial women.

Fictional role models influence the behavior of millennial women as well.

Television's *Buffy the Vampire Slayer* (The WB/UPN), which aired from 1997 to 2003, exerted a powerful influence on young millennial women. Joss Whedon created Buffy as an empowered woman—strong, savvy, and sexy. Buffy, with the help of her friends, battled evil while coping with the ups and downs of high school. Millennials identified with Buffy and her ongoing battle to fight for good with friends by her side.

The lead character in the 1998 Walt Disney film *Mulan*, which was based on the Chinese legend of Hua Mulan, was a young woman who disguised herself as a man so she could go to war in place of her father. To millennial fans, Mulan is the cool young woman who saved China. McDonald's featured her as their first international Happy Meal toy.

J. K. Rowling's Harry Potter novels and films were a significant influence on millennial women during their formative years. While Harry is the star, Hermione, witch extraordinaire and Harry's best friend, is an advocate for the better treatment of house elves and a fighter in the Battle of Hogwarts.

As always happens in generational history, similar characteristic-forming influences and events pop up in different ways from the beginning of a generation to the end of a generation. An example is *The Hunger Games* trilogy by Suzanne Collins, which debuted in 2008. The series' fictional heroine, sixteen-year-old Katniss Everdeen, is a Hunger Games winner—a warrior and a strong role model for young millennial women who buy her tough-girl action toys as well as Hunger Games earrings, earbuds, and Lego sets.

The media hypes Britney Spears, Miley Cyrus, and the Kardashians, but the most influential millennial role models tend to be women who are strong and empowered.

Advertising that connects with millennial women's values will attract them to your products and services. Millennials' role models, both real and fictional, exemplify these values.

5

Athletics! Big Ideas! Math and Science!

Millennial women expect marketers to see them as very different from other generations.

For the first time in U.S. history, American girls and young women see themselves as physically strong.

Millennials are the first generation of American women to fully reap the benefits of Title IX, the federal legislation that guarantees equal funding for sports to both women and men in colleges and other institutions that receive public money. Being athletic is a major part of the modern American girls' and women's lifestyle. Here's how business is taking advantage of Title IX's influence:

- An advertisement for Neutrogena Deep Clean Pore Strips featured a young girl wearing boxing gloves.

- The Indianapolis 500 featured millennial race car driver Danica Patrick, the first woman to win an IndyCar series race. She is now a worldwide celebrity.

- Companies of all sizes support millennial women's athletic events.

Millennial women feel they can do and be anything.

In 2004, millennial Erin Feehan-Nelson, at the age of seventeen, ran for mayor of her town of St. Mary's Point, Minnesota. Her campaign slogan was "Uncorrupted by years of experience." She didn't win, but her efforts were typical of an empowered millennial. Fast forward to the 2014 congressional elections. Thirty-year-old millennial Elise Stefanik won New York State's 21st Congressional District to become the youngest woman ever to serve in Congress.

Then there's millennial Alexandra Scott from Pennsylvania, who, while she was undergoing treatment for cancer at the age of four, decided to do something to raise money for cancer research. She opened a lemonade stand in front of her home, and contributed all proceeds to cancer research. That action became a national drive called Alex's Lemonade Stand for Childhood Cancer which had raised almost $200K by the time Alexandra passed away four years later in 2004. In her memory, several jewelry designers created "lemonade" jewelry, which sells on QVC. Her efforts continue today, even expanding into the sale of "lemonade" candy at grocery stores.

Not all millennial women will be a congresswoman at age thirty or a fundraiser at age four, but the stories of those that are, represent the millennial can-do attitude.

Millennials have changed women's attitudes toward math, science, and technology.

In the past, technology studies and occupations were dominated by males. Times have changed. Now, millennial women are drawn to tech companies and tech jobs.

The Federal Government encourages students to pursue studies in technological fields in part because the threat of terrorism has led to the need for jobs in cyber security.

Television also promotes women's interests in science, with network and cable shows featuring women in prominent roles. TV's trend of focusing on scientific subjects has created popular female role models such as *Covert Affairs'* (USA Network) fashionista/CIA spy Annie Walker, *CSI's* (CBS) agent Catherine Willows, and *NCIS'* (CBS) female agent millennial Ellie Bishop and forensic scientist Abby Sciuto.

CSI: Crime Scene Investigation (CBS) has been a millennial favorite. In 2012, the show was named the most watched show in the world for the fifth time. Businesses are discovering and developing opportunities such as CSI-inspired scientific activities at children's summer camps.

The primary technology driver, however, is capitalism. In the information age, tech entrepreneurs are the new rock stars. Google and Intel offer scholarships to tech-minded young men and women. L'Oréal develops opportunities for women scientists by offering grants.

Time Warner Cable's "Connect a Million Minds" initiative has offered $100 million to address America's declining proficiency in science, technology, engineering, and math (STEM) so that America's young people will be able to compete more successfully globally. Millennials are responding!

Millennials are redefining the image of the American woman. She is physically strong, full of big ideas, and tech-savvy.

6

Millennial Women Believe in Themselves, Feminism, and Multi-tasking

---

Millennial women are ultra, ultra confident.

Millennial **Divya Nag** from El Dorado Hills, California, cofounded Stem Cell Theranostics and StartX Med, two initiatives that attempt to solve the problem of keeping human cells alive in a petri dish so that testing new drugs can be less risky, less costly, and less time consuming.[15]

Millennial **Meg Gill** from Chester, Virginia, is the youngest female brewery owner in the country, and Gill's Los Angeles-based company, Golden Road Brewing, is one of the fastest-growing craft beer companies in the U.S.[16]

Millennial **Kim Swift** from Seattle was in college when she and some classmates created the puzzle game that eventually became Portal, which has since sold in the millions.[17]

Millennial **Lily DeBell**, an eighth grader from Baltimore, in response to her younger sister's need for comfortable legwarmers for dance class, started a company called Lily's

Legwarmers–knitted products made with organic wool and Alpaca fleece. (Her grandmother taught her how to knit.) She now sells the legwarmers on Etsy, an e-commerce site connecting buyers and sellers of handmade and vintage items.

Millennial women live the feminist movement's goals, control their own lives, and do almost everything their male counterparts do.

They are both behind the scenes and on the front lines in wars. According to the Department of Defense, in 2013, there were over two hundred thousand women serving in the military, representing nearly 15% of the fighting force.[18]

And, in increasing numbers, millennial women are choosing to be stay-at-home moms.[19] One explanation is that millennial mothers feel strongly about the stay-at-home effect on children. The "Soccer Moms" of past generations have become the "Security Moms" of the millennial generation. These security moms seek out ways to best protect and educate their children. Home schooling is growing at rates seven times faster than the number of children enrolling in grades K-12 each year.[20]

Millennial women are increasingly the family breadwinner. In 2013, 40% of American households with children under age eighteen included a mother who is either the sole or primary earner for her family, according to Pew Research Center.[21]

Millennials excel at multi-tasking.

This is their norm. Millennials have grown up with computers, cellphones, and tablets.

Here's a snapshot of a given moment in the life of an early-wave millennial: She's on the speaker phone, the television is on, music is playing in the background, she's simultaneously surfing the net and text-messaging her vote for an *American Idol* contestant, and all the while still carrying on a phone conversation.[22] She grew up in a five-hundred-television-channel universe.

What is normal to younger millennials is exemplified well by Roku, a company that makes TV set-top boxes that stream 200K+ movies and TV episodes on demand via the Internet. Even their pets have their own channel.

Multi-tasking millennials are tied to the Internet. They are incapable of getting information and entertainment the way they want it via traditional means such as newspapers and television. TV usage among viewers age eighteen to thirty-four is falling.[23] "The change in behavior is stunning. The use of streaming and smartphones just year-on-year is double-digit increases," says Alan Wurtzel, NBCUniversal's audience research chief in a *New York Post* interview.[24]

Millennials, more than any other generation, receive an enormous number of messages every day, and they thrive on it. To reach busy millennials, speak their language, as Chase Bank did in a campaign where they displayed signs in branch windows that read "Gt $ fstr" ("Get money faster").

Because millennials are multi-taskers—at home, at work, and while shopping—marketers can reach them via websites, social networks, television, radio, mobile devices, streaming video, and even on bank windows. Marketing and promotion has to come from more than one direction.

The same goes for shopping. Millennial women want the buzz, the experience, the thrill of the hunt, the deal, the visuals, *and* the service. So give them what they want and use more than one method to do it!

The bottom line is, you are dealing with very confident women who are champion multi-taskers.

7

Millennials' Idiosyncrasies Are Many, and They Impact Your Company and Sales

Every generation has idiosyncrasies. Millennials are no exception. Their unique behavior can be a major problem to employers, as they will require more training than other generations.

Millennial women's behavior is often inappropriate.

To millennial women, it's not about breaking rules; it's about not knowing the rules or not caring about them. In fact, they tend to do their own thing in spite of protocol or good form. As an example, in 2005, the Northwestern University national championship women's lacrosse team was invited to visit the White House to meet President Bush. Many on the team wore flip-flops—shoes more suitable for the beach or a casual bar.

The flip-flop flap seems like a small thing now, but it signaled to other generations that millennials didn't understand appropriate fashion for the occasion. Such are millennials—they do not fully understand many societal norms.

These millennial women defended the footwear they chose to wear to the White House by saying the beach sandals were an appropriately dressy shoe because they were nice flip-flops, and some styles even had rhinestones on them!

In the business world, Clifford Chance, a prestigious global law firm, felt compelled to send a five-page guide to female employees in its New York and Washington, D.C., offices listing behavioral tips. Here are a few from its 163-point memo: don't giggle; wear a suit, not your party outfit; don't show cleavage; lose the "um," "uh," "you know," and "like"; if wearing a skirt, make sure the audience can't see up it when sitting on the dais.[25]

Millennial women have developed their own definition of what they perceive as appropriate. Conversely, millennial women have a tough time understanding what others consider appropriate. They model themselves after women on TV, like reporters and actresses, many of whom appear in a workplace environment dressed as sex objects. Millennials mimic music performers who act outrageously. They model themselves after mothers and grandmothers who pursue a youthful lifestyle.

Millennials are unconcerned with privacy. They are the tell-all generation.

Millennials' lack of concern about privacy can be beneficial to marketers. If your company does something that pleases a millennial customer, she will tell her friends and anyone else who will listen to her.

But, if you displease a millennial, prepare for her wrath! While the Facebook generation can be your best publicist, it can also be your worst nightmare. Millennials don't think twice about trashing your product, your service, and you personally. They'll do it via every means available, starting with social media. They live in a water cooler world where nothing is off limits when it comes to gossip.

More than any other generation in American history, most millennial employees do not understand their responsibility to the companies for whom they work. Issues with discretion are commonly a challenge for younger generations, but it's worse with millennials. For marketers and businesses that employ millennials, guiding them begins on day one. Millennial employees:

- who represent you must be trained in what is appropriate both inside and outside the company.

- need coaching in good manners and etiquette, both personal and professional.

- should not have access to private information until it is clear they can be trusted.

- who work in critical or sensitive positions must have thorough background checks to ensure your trade secrets will be protected! (Example: Edward Snowden.)

- have a short attention span, so break down long assignments into smaller segments.

- need constant praise, given that they are accustomed to getting sports trophies just for participation, not achievement.

- don't understand that they are out in the real world facing real-world demands.

Millennials are products of the information age.

In general, millennials lack the ability to communicate face-to-face. They're accustomed to tweeting, texting, emailing, and calling. They rarely have their heads up from their mobile devices. They often seem unaware of, or unable to, read body language, verbal signals or facial cues. Digital is their native language.

Millennial women expect businesses to understand and adapt to their lifestyle. Here are some ways to meet their expectations:

Millennials tend to bond to products and services at a young age. Even if your product is not on the millennial buy list today, it's still important that they know your brand. There are many ways you can do that. If it's possible, invite young millennials to visit your company on a field trip. Silicon Valley tech companies roll out the red carpet for talented teenage interns by offering good pay and free concerts. Other ways to reach them is by donating money to their school or having your employees mentor them. Fidelity Investments, for example, creates volunteer opportunities for employees to use their knowledge to teach students how to make smart financial decisions. By engaging millennials, you influence their friends as well, so your touch goes further.

Depending on your products and services, millennials expect to be acknowledged at every stage of their lives. They expect you to be there for them during their college life, job searches, wedding, home hunting and furnishing, raising a family, etc.

Millennial women expect to be part of a company's product development and marketing outreach. For example, Frito-Lay's annual "Do Us A Flavor" contest invites people to create the next great potato chip. In 2012, Frito-Lay's "Do Us A Flavor" Facebook page averaged 22.5 million visits per week, and that year's sales increased by 12%. Frito-Lay's marketing strategy is an example of inclusive product development and focused marketing, which millennials love.[26]

In the perfume industry, Oscar de la Renta turned to his stepdaughter for inspiration before he used Facebook to help launch his first new fragrance in ten years. He gave those who *liked* the new perfume, "Esprit d'Oscar," a free sample.

Dior uses a millennial-sensitive app to promote their products. The app offers lessons in style and tutorials on makeup application.

Other fragrance companies align themselves with well-known women millennials recognize, such as Sarah Jessica Parker, millennials' first fashion muse. Parker was asked by Coty to create her own perfume. It's "Lovely"! Many fragrances are endorsed by celebrities millennials know: Britney Spears' scent "Curious," Kim Kardashian's namesake scent, Jennifer Lopez's "Glow," and Beyoncé's "Heat."

Millennial women expect to have input in the development or marketing of your product or service.

The idiosyncrasies of millennials are many, and knowing them will impact your sales.

If You're Not Familiar with These Seven Trends, You're Already Behind

The trends of a given generation are molded by the historic events that occurred during that generation's formative years.

Consider these seven important millennial trends.

1. Millennial women are physically strong, like no generation before them.

Millennial women don't care for gender stereotypes like the one featured in a 2015 Super Bowl commercial called "Don't throw like a girl." Millennial women can handle physically demanding jobs, and companies recognize this and are hiring them as truck drivers, luggage handlers, and construction workers.

2. Millennial women are redefining motherhood.

Millennials can be stay-at-home moms or breadwinners. And, an increasing number of young American women are choosing to care for pets over children. This trend has caught the attention of diverse sources. In 2013, *Time* ran a cover story titled "The Childfree Life."[27] Blue Buffalo Pet Food understands this trend and, in some of their commercials, markets their products specifically to pet parents. In 2014, in an attempt to counter the trend, Pope Francis urged married couples to raise children, not dogs and cats.

3. Being single is an acceptable millennial lifestyle.

Millennials marry later than the three previous generations. A Pew Research Center survey found that only 26% of millennials (aged eighteen to thirty-three in 2014) were married.[28] This is quite a contrast from prior generations. The millennial singles market is an attractive opportunity not to be ignored!

Leslie Gillock, Vice President of Wray Ward ad agency, highlights this trend in an article called "Single Americans and Home Ownership." She points out that singles account for more than half the American adult population for the first time. Nearly one-third of homebuyers in 2013 were not married. Almost half of millennial women value home ownership above getting married and having children.[29]

4. Millennials want to give their time as well as their money to charities.

At the time of the writing of this book, Tulane University offered a program called India 2015: Compassion in Action. The program offers students an opportunity to spend four weeks in India involved in community service and social work projects. Closer to home, Tulane students can volunteer to build homes in New Orleans through Habitat for Humanity; promote social inclusion by becoming a Best Buddy to a person with intellectual and developmental disabilities, and help that person explore opportunities; visit people in nursing homes and rehabilitation centers; train service dogs; or work on urban farms.

And, millennials want to know how charities will use their money and they also want to be involved in disbursement decisions. A report from Millennial Impact, an initiative for organizations to learn how to best engage the millennial generation through research, found that millennials are not interested in institutions or structures, but rather in people. A contribution to a millennial-favored charity that helps people in need will benefit you, too.[30]

5. Millennials embrace ethnic and lifestyle diversity.

According to a Pew Research Center survey:[31] 68% of millennials feel same-sex couples should be allowed to marry, 69% support the legalization of marijuana, and 55% feel undocumented immigrants should be allowed to stay and apply for citizenship.

These statistics are reflected in today's TV shows and commercials because marketers are responding to them. Millennials are a major segment of TV's most sought-after 18-to-49-year-old demographic audience.

6. Millennials are suspicious of marketing efforts. Trust must be earned.

When asked the question "Generally speaking, would you say that most people can be trusted or that you can't be too careful in dealing with people," only 19% of millennials say most people can be trusted.[32] It is apparent businesses must earn their trust.

- Use social media sites that best connect your product or service to the targeted millennial consumer. For example, Pinterest is the go-to place for fashion, accessories, special occasion clothing, and casual clothing.[33] Your message must come from several directions—not just one—but it's worth figuring out which those are.

- Train your salespeople to understand the importance of every millennial sales encounter. This is vital, because millennials not only dish the dirt, they also share the hottest product information with friends and broadcast it on social media.

- Reward millennial loyalty—give them special discounts for bringing friends along to shop.

- Create a website that is clean, easy-to-navigate, and interactive. Millennials want good visuals and little copy. Too many sales are lost by poor, unappealing websites. Millennials think: "If they don't understand how to create a good website, how can they possibly understand me?" Don't become known as the company with the dated website.

7. Millennials have the ability to unify a divided America.

Millennials value the good of a group over the needs of an individual. Working together is a big part of their generational DNA.

Today we are a divided America as a result of the fallout from the attitudes of previous generations. For example: Baby Boomers (born 1943 to 1960)[34] focused on, and still focus on, the individual over the group. Their mantra is "It's all about me." In contrast, millennials think in terms of the group over the individual. They are frustrated by divisions in sex, race, religion, politics, age, experience, status, and wealth.

Millennials are the modern-day version of America's greatest generation—the World War II generation (born 1901 to 1924)[35] that brought us out of the dust bowl, the Great Depression, and World War II.

Millennials are the can-do kids whose trends will change the course of America.

Advertising: You Have Five Seconds to Make Your Point

Advertising to millennial women means meeting their expectations.

Attracting millennials is not what attracting customers used to be. Modern teens depend on social networks and mobile video. They watch only about twenty-one hours of TV per week, as compared to older generations, who watch about forty-nine hours.[36] Less television watched means fewer TV commercials seen.

Television commercials typically fill thirty- and sixty-second slots. Millennials, however, are accustomed to the shorter advertising common on the Internet. They'll pay attention, but they have a short attention span. You have five seconds to intrigue them or to make your initial argument. Often, if you look at the most successful millennial spots, the first five seconds is the spot! Just look at any good YouTube video.

Super Bowl TV commercials are still highly anticipated by millennials (as they are by all viewers), but how do companies target them the rest of the time? The answer is: via their mobile device. In 2013, 70% of millennials aged thirteen to seventeen, and 79% of millennials aged eighteen to twenty-four, already had smart phones.[37] The average teenager sends more than sixty text messages a day, while many send more than that.[38] Just imagine how many they receive!

Millennials want their phones to be for personal use, not invasive advertising, so there's a balance to strike. A USC Annenberg/Bovitz survey found that millennials show more interest in cooperating with Internet businesses as long as they receive something tangible in return.[39] If a millennial wants to purchase flowers, she can ask her phone to tell her if there is a flower shop in the area. Google Now, an intelligent personal assistant mobile app, tells her if a product she's been searching for online is available at a nearby store.[40]

The Millennial woman expects cool and new products.

Target has been one of the millennial woman's favorite places to shop. Target's team of trend-spotters researches and travels the world to find great, new products. Their marketing strategy is to offer what is chic, novel, and edgy, yet reasonably priced—from designer dresses to whimsical teakettles. Shopping for products at Target is a millennial adventure.

In 2011, Target launched a collection from the Italian design house Missoni, featuring Missoni-For-Target clothing, home décor, and kitchenware. A millennial woman could redo her wardrobe or her dorm room with Missoni's hallmark zigzags and swirls. The Missoni promotion was supposed to last six weeks, but items sold out at most stores and online in just one day.

Millennials are attracted to products that are environmentally safe.

An example is Charles Viancin's Lilypad® silicone lids. Lilypad® lids take the place of plastic wrap and are environmentally safe. They also make the inside of the fridge look good—all things that appeal to millennials.

Millennial women expect speed like no other generation of women before them.

As early as 2006, some companies began to recognize the need for speed, so businesses made an effort to speed things up.[41] Consider the following: Chase Bank cut transaction time for getting cash from forty-two seconds to twenty-four; Walmart redesigned its website to enable customers to buy in four clicks instead of six; Amazon.com delivers thousands of everyday essential items to areas of Manhattan in one hour and offers free two-day shipping as part of their Amazon Prime service; and, the Federal Aviation Administration has given Amazon permission to test drones that will make Prime service deliveries within thirty minutes to addresses located within ten miles of its warehouses.[42]

The Millennial woman wants to trust the companies she deals with. When trust is broken, shopping stops.

This generation has been bombarded with marketing messages all their lives, so they know hype when they see and hear it. A study from the McCarthy Group called *Engaging Millennials: Trust and Attention Survey* says millennials trust their closest friends first, news reports and social network friends second, company websites third, and only as a last resort do they look at advertising and sales pitches. Eighty-four percent of millennials do not trust advertising![43]

The key to gaining trust with the millennial woman is providing:

- Consistent product quality (like Apple)
- Fair transaction practices (like QVC's no-questions-asked return policy)
- Fulfillment of marketing promises (like Chipotle's quality food promise)
- A place to vote or voice meaningful opinions (like Amazon's customer ratings and TV's *The Voice*'s audience interaction)

The millennial woman sees herself as part of the show.

Twitter, Facebook, and Instagram have become the digital water coolers of the millennial generation, according to ABC Family's president Michael Riley. In an *Ad Age* article,[44] Riley said, when giving a definition of young viewers, "We sum it up in one really long word: television-viewing-fan-tweeting-app-using-blog-discussing-text-chatting-mobile-watching-consumers."

In 2013, ABC Family's TV series *Pretty Little Liars* was the top-rated show among female millennials, who used Twitter to talk both to each other about the show and to the show directly. In fact, this TV show was the most frequently tweeted-about television series.[45] Tweeting about a brand bonds millennials to a brand.

Scandal (ABC), a political thriller set in Washington, D.C., is regularly at the top of the eighteen to thirty-four-year-old demographic. Jeff Fromm of *Ad Age* attributes its success in part to social media outreach from the series' stars who tweet about the show regularly.[46] Tweeting has become such a part of the *Scandal* viewing experience for millennials, they try to watch it live, and that means commercials may not get skipped.

The millennial woman expects first-rate service and a little pampering.

Millennials expect a company to track their past purchases, to know if they prefer updates via text or email, and to learn from their shopping interests. That's before they purchase. After they buy, millennials want to be able to give instant feedback on the products they purchased and their shopping experiences.

The millennial woman demands personalized retail service similar to what luxury store Bergdorf Goodman provides. A Bergdorf's salesperson, armed with a customer's buying history, calls the customer who purchased grey slacks the year before to tell her that the perfect sweater for those slacks has just arrived. When the customer comes into Bergdorf's, the salesperson ushers her into a dressing room to see the new sweater along with coordinating shoes, jackets, and scarves.

Similarly, Amazon tracks a customer's purchases and

searches, then suggests additional complementary merchandise. That's personalized retail service, "new-style." It has made Amazon a leader in interactive marketing and site stickiness (That's how many minutes per month the average visitor spends on their website).

The millennial woman expects a business to communicate in her style, which is digital.

Millennials are the first generation of consumers to grow up in a digital world and they expect you to communicate digitally, whether by phone, tablet, watch, or game console.

Capital Group, one of the world's largest investment managers, expects even more millennial dollars to be spent online in the future for all sorts of goods and services.[47] So, speaking "digital" can make a significant difference in sales.

Domino's and Papa John's communicate to millennials through ads and commercials that invite them to order pizza and other food items online. These two companies enjoyed a 40% or more increase in sales in 2013.[48]

The millennial woman expects companies and businesses to understand and connect to her everyday lifestyle.

Jell-O brought its brand into the millennial age with a successful ad campaign. Using the information from Twitter feeds, Jell-O created a Mood Monitor to advertise its pudding products to millennials. The Mood Monitor counts the number of *smilies* and *frownies* being tweeted, and if there are more frowns than smiles, Jell-O offers a coupon for free pudding to some of the sad-face tweeters. In the first week of the marketing campaign, Jell-O's Twitter feed received 55 million tweets.[49]

Smaller companies can find creative ways to be part of a millennial's life too. Businesses in college towns can offer promotions that coincide with the first day on campus, study week, exam time, sorority events, date nights, athletic events, parents' weekend, and graduation.

The millennial woman is socially conscious and expects businesses to promote the welfare of others.

Forbes says that 32% of millennials have stopped buying from companies that have social practices they find unacceptable.[50] The following companies represent a new type of corporate social responsibility—one that appeals to millennials.

Whole Foods Market supports causes that make sense for its company culture, from trying to save disappearing colonies of honeybees to helping provide salad bars in school cafeterias. They employ a lot of millennials, and Whole Foods has become the luxury grocery brand for millennial shoppers, who are health-conscious and have a taste for the exotic.

The Nike Foundation helped create a movement called The Girl Effect, which encourages adolescent girls to end poverty for themselves, their families, their communities, their countries, and the world. Its programs reach out to girls in need everywhere and range from supplying feminine hygiene products so that girls feel comfortable attending school every day of the month to stopping child marriages to enabling young entrepreneurs to develop wider markets. While The Girl Effect provides tremendous resources, it is also about encouraging adolescent girls to become part of the larger effort to end poverty for young women around the world.

Jeff Fromm (*Ad Age*) explains the importance of corporate responsibility this way: ". . . millennials will seek out and buy brands that support a cause that aligns with their values."[51] Fromm adds that when a millennial woman buys from companies that stand for causes she cares about, she feels better about herself.

Millennial advertising checklist

- ☑ Meet her expectations
- ☑ Advertise cool, new products
- ☑ Advertise environmentally safe products
- ☑ Offer fast service
- ☑ Build trust with every purchase
- ☑ Give her first-rate service
- ☑ Advertise where millennials go to look
- ☑ Communicate her way–digitally
- ☑ Connect to her everyday life
- ☑ Let her know your company cares about people

10

Success Stories: Companies That Connect with Millennial Women

Millennials seek something from businesses that America's five other generations do not. They want a product, a service, and a brand that represents and identifies with their lives.

Companies that have studied millennials are reaping the rewards. Here are some of the brands that have unraveled the millennial mystery to win them over.

Moosylvania.com, an independent ad agency released its Millennials' 2015 Favorite Brands Ranking Report.[52] The top ten brands:

1. Nike	6. Target
2. Apple	7. Microsoft
3. Samsung	8. Coca-Cola
4. Sony	9. Air Jordan
5. Walmart	10. Pepsi

In 2014, *Business Insider* (a business and technology news website) cited **Goldman Sachs** and *Teen Vogue*'s list of 50 brands that young women love most.[53] The top ten:

1. Forever 21
2. PINK Victoria's Secret
3. Victoria's Secret
4. eos
5. Target
6. Converse
7. Sephora
8. H&M
9. Urban Outfitters
10. Nike

In 2013, **Vision Critical's BERA Group** ranked these ten brands and products top among millennials:[54]

1. Google
2. YouTube
3. Amazon
4. Nintendo
5. Oreo
6. Microsoft
7. Reese's
8. iPod
9. Crayola
10. Google Chrome

Millennial women gravitate to products, services, and brands that identify with their lives. Here are a few companies that understand this:

American Girl (www.americangirl.com) sells dolls, clothes, games, and gifts. This company connects with millennials at a very young age. That's important because millennials often bond to brands early and for life.

Build-A-Bear (www.buildabear.com) offers a high level of interactivity, teaching young girls how to build their own bears.

Urban Outfitters (www.urbanoutfitters.com) is a destination shopping experience that is entertaining to millennials. Their stores are lifestyle centers full of new merchandise. Their website offers the latest music, fashion advice, and apartment decorating tips.

Macy's (www.macys.com) is redesigning an entire floor in its Manhattan store to appeal to its millennial customers.

Target (www.target.com) offers merchandise by hot young designers at low prices. Target made *Fast Company*'s top ten list of Most Innovative Companies of 2013 for creating City Target stores, which are stocked with inventory that appeals to millennial apartment dwellers.

Dove (www.dove.us) understands the real millennial woman, and created the Dove Campaign for Real Beauty in 2004.

Stage one of their campaign placed Dove billboard ads in major cities around the world. The billboards featured famed photographer Annie Leibovitz's photographs of everyday women, not professional models. One billboard photograph pictured a not-so-skinny woman, and passers-by could vote online for Fat or Fab. A running tally of votes was displayed on an interactive billboard in Times Square (NYC). The purpose of the campaign was to challenge how women define real beauty.

Stage two featured a series of Dove TV spots and print ads, which culminated in a Super Bowl TV commercial.

Stage three featured viral Dove videos. One called "Sketches" highlighted how women saw themselves as contrasted to how other people saw them. It became one of the most-watched viral video ads with 15 million views in the first week alone.

To commemorate the tenth anniversary of the Dove Campaign for Real Beauty, Dove created a short film called "Selfie" that featured girls and their mothers discussing their insecurities and at the same time snapping an honest selfie photo. That film went viral as well.

QVC (www.qvc.com) encouraged millennial women to play a major role in a marketing campaign called "Courtney says 'I do'." The marketing collaboration between QVC and *Southern Living* magazine invited millennials to have a voice in helping QVC show hostess Courtney Cason plan her dream wedding. Viewers voted on everything from appetizers to centerpieces to wedding favors. On Courtney's QVC page (and blog), millennial women learned everything they would need for their own weddings.

Courtyard by Marriott (www.marriott.com) has redesigned its Courtyard by Marriott brand for millennials who want something different and authentic, that they can text and tweet about, such as locally made potato chips and beer in the minibar, artwork by locals on the wall, a Swedish deejay spinning on the hotel's rooftop bar, a local underground wine bar with a secret entrance, and bistro lobbies with pod seating to encourage socializing.

Kimpton (www.kimptonhotels.com) wants to make the single female business traveler feel right at home at their hotels. Their "Women in Touch" program includes complimentary tote bags containing yoga equipment to aid guests who want to follow along on the hotel's yoga TV channel. The hotels also provide eye makeup remover pads and hand-held clothing steamers. The Kimpton chain welcomes pets (a millennial favorite). They offer digital access to a performance coach and wellness experts, and there's a special menu created just for women.

In late 2014, InterContinental Hotels Group, one of the world's largest hoteliers, bought Kimpton Hotels to increase its exposure to millennials via the fast-growing boutique hotel sector.

Converse (www.converse.com) maintains its appeal from generation to generation. In its ads, commercials, and YouTube videos, the brand remains authentic to its philosophy of highlighting the creative lifestyle of its customers who wear Converse sneakers rather than highlighting just its shoes. To attract millennials, their lifestyle becomes an important part of the branding as in one Converse commercial that shows the world of the millennial woman running at dawn or getting home at dawn or kissing her boyfriend at the grocery store.

Another millennial favorite is the fact that Converse invites customers to become artists by using their sneakers as a blank canvas on which they personalize the shoe's design.

IKEA (www.ikea.com) and **Delta Airlines** (www.delta-air.com) have created products and services that show an understanding of the extreme devotion millennials have for their pets. Ikea designed a combination sofa/cat scratcher called KÄT. Cats can sharpen their claws without harming the sofa. Delta now offers the first pet-tracking device. Since accompanying pets are flying in a different part of the plane, the GPS device allows flyers to check on the temperature surrounding their pet as well as their pet's position (sleeping, sitting, or upside-down).

Millennial women want companies to understand their real lives.

Conclusion

Millennial women are a marketer's delight.

Millennials love to shop and they love to talk about shopping. To have millennial women say good things about your company, your products, your services, and your service also means they unlock their pocketbooks.

Exit questions

[?] Does your company have the generational knowledge to connect with millennial women?

[?] Are you able to cut through the communication overload so that your company's message is heard?

[?] How can your company win the hearts and minds of millennial women?

Understanding this generation of consumers requires revisiting how to capture them. But then, forty million millennial women are a coveted market. It pays to get to know them.

NOTES

1   Geoff Johns, *Infinite Crisis* (New York: DC Comics, 2006) 34.

2   Jonathan Vespa, U.S. Census Bureau, personal interview, Jul-Aug. 2014.

3   Ibid.

4   "Supplier Responsibility," *Apple,* n.d. Web. <https://www.apple.com/supplier-responsibility/environment/>.

5   Sally Seppanen and Wendy Gualtieri, "The Millennial Generation Research Review," *U.S. Chamber of Commerce Foundation,* 14 Nov. 2012. Web. <http://www.uschamberfoundation.org/millennial-generation-research-review>.

6   William Strauss and Neil Howe, *Generations: The History of America's Future,* 1584 to 2069 (New York: Quill William Morrow, cop., 1991) 338.

7   Ibid.

8   Quote from Ahu Arslan Yildiz, 2014 UNESCO-L'Olréal Fellow, L'Oréal Corporate Foundation, n.d. Web. <http://www.loreal.com/csr-commitments/foundation/science/women-and-scientific-excellence>.

9   Anu Jessy, "Top 15 Most Popular Social Networking Sites–June 2014," *Free Social Media,* 10 Jun 2014. Web. <http://freesocialmarketing.blogspot.com/2014/06/top-15-most-popular-social-networking.html>.

10   Fast Company staff, "The World's Top 10 Most Innovative Companies in Social Media," *Fast Company*, n.d. Web. <http://www.fastcompany.com/3026321/most-innovative-companies-2014/the-worlds-top-10-most-innovative-companies-in-social-media>.

11   Ilya Pozan, "20 Companies You Should Be Following on Social Media," *Forbes*, 6 Mar. 2014. Web. <http://www.forbes.com/sites/ilyapozin/2014/03/06/20-companies-you-should-be-following-on-social-media/>.

12   Kate Taylor, "The 10 Best Websites for Millennial Women 2013," *Forbes*, 21 Aug. 2013. Web. <http://www.forbes.com/pictures/ffhm45eemm/the-10-best-websites-for-millennial-women-2013-2/>.

13   NetBase press release, "NetBase Retail Report: Millennials Don't See Facebook as the Top Source of Inspiration for Fashion Purchases," *NetBase*, 13 Nov. 2013. Web. <http://www.netbase.com/press-release/netbase-retail-report-millennials-dont-see-facebook-as-the-top-source-of-inspiration-for-fashion-purchases/>.

14   Alina Dizik, "Ordering Jeans Straight, With a Touch of Stretch," *The Wall Street Journal*, 11 Nov. 2010. Web. <http://online.wsj.com/articles/SB10001424052748703805004575606533495860918>.

15   Matthew Herper and Andrea Navarro, "Forbes 30 under 30: Science & Healthcare," *Forbes*, n.d. Web. <http://www.forbes.com/special-report/2014/30-under-30/science-and-healthcare.html>.

16   Vanna Le, "Forbes 30 Under 30: Food & Drink," *Forbes*, 6 Jan. 2014. Web. <http://www.forbes.com/pictures/eimi45eelh/meg-gill-28/>.

17   David M. Ewalt, "30 under 30: The Brightest Young Stars in Video Games," *Forbes*, 12 Dec. 2012. Web. <http://www.forbes.com/pictures/mlg45lhig/kim-swift/>.

18   Leon E. Panetta, Secretary of Defense Speech, "Statement on Women in Service," *U.S. Department of Defense*, 24 Jan. 2013. Web. <http://www.defense.gov/speeches/speech.aspx?speechid=1746>.

19 D'Vera Cohn, Gretchen Livingston, and Wendy Wang, "After Decades of
     Decline, A Rise in Stay-at-Home Mothers," Pew Research *Social &
     Demographic Trends*, 8 Apr. 2014. Web. <http://www.pewsocial
     trends.org/2014/04/08/after-decades-of-decline-a-rise-in-stay-
     at-home-mothers/>.

20 Julia Lawrence, "Number of Homeschoolers Growing Nationwide,"
     Education News, 21 May 2012. Web. <http://www.educationnews.
     org/parenting/number-of-homeschoolers-growing-nationwide>.

21 Wendy Wang, Kim Parker, and Paul Taylor, "Breadwinner Moms,"
     Pew Research *Social & Demographic Trends*, 29 May 2013.
     Web. <http://www.pewsocialtrends.org/2013/05/29/breadwinner-
     moms/>.

22 Descriptive elements from an unknown source.

23 Claire Atkinson, "Millennials ditching their TV sets at a record rate,"
     New York Post, 16 Feb. 2015. Web. <http://nypost.com/2015/02/16/
     millenials-ditching-their-tv-sets-at-a-record-rate/>.

24 Ibid.

25 Daily Mail Reporter, "Top law firm sends email to female employees
     telling them to 'practice hard words' and to stop giggling or
     showing their cleavage," *Daily Mail.com*, 25 Oct. 2013.
     Web. <http://www.dailymail.co.uk/news/article-2477083/Top-law-
     firm-sends-email-female-employees-telling-learn-hard-words-
     stop-giggling-showing-cleavage.html>.

26 "Frito-Lay's Do Us a Flavor–Gold," *Chief Marketer*, n.d.
     Web. <https://blog.instant.ly/blog/2014/08/lays-2013-do-us-a-
     flavor-contest-value-intelligent-concept-testing/>.

27 Lauren Sandler, "Having It All Without Having Children," *Time*,
     12 Aug. 2013. Web. <http://time.com/241/having-it-all-without-
     having-children/>.

28 Bruce Drake, "6 new findings about Millennials," *Pew Research Center,*
    7 Mar. 2014. Web. <http://www.pewresearch.org/fact-tank/
    2014/03/07/6-new-findings-about-millennials/>.

29 Leslie Gillock, "Single Americans and Home Ownership," 24 Nov. 2014.
    Blog. <http://www.wrayward.com/blog/2014/11/single-americans-
    and-home-ownership>.

30 "Inspiring the Next Generation Workforce," *The 2014 Millennial Impact
    Report,* n.d. Online report. <http://www.pointsoflight.org/sites/
    default/files/resources/files/2014_millennial_impact_report.pdf>.

31 "Millennials in Adulthood, Chapter 2: Generations and Issues,"
    Pew Research Center *Social & Demographic Trends,* 7 Mar. 2014.
    Web. <http://www.pewsocialtrends.org/2014/03/07/chapter-2-
    generations-and-issues/>.

32 Drake, "6 new findings about Millennials" (see note 29).

33 NetBase press release, "NetBase Retail Report: Millennials Don't See
    Facebook as the Top Source of Inspiration for Fashion Purchases"
    (see note 14).

34 Strauss and Howe, Generations: *The History of America's Future*
    (see note 7).

35 Ibid.

36 Jeff Fromm, "Millennials Study Provides New Data on Media, Shopping
    and Social Habits," *Barkley,* 18 Aug. 2011. Web. <http://blog.
    barkleyus.com/2011/08/18/millennials-study-provides-new-data-
    on-media-shopping-and-social-habits/>.

37 Nielson, "Ring the Bells: More Smartphones in Students' Hand Ahead of
    Back-to-School Season," *Nielson,* 29 Oct. 2013. Web. <http://www.
    nielsen.com/us/en/insights/news/2013/ring-the-bells-more-
    smartphones-in-students-hands-ahead-of-back.html>.

38 Amanda Lenhart, "Teens, Smartphones & Texting," *Pew Research Center Internet, Science & Tech,* 19 Mar. 2012. Web. <http://www.pewinternet.org/2012/03/19/teens-smartphones-texting/>.

39 "Is online privacy over? Findings from the USC Annenberg Center for the Digital Future show Millennials embrace a new online reality," *USC Annenberg School For Communication and Journalism,* 22 Apr. 2013. Web. <http://annenberg.usc.edu/News%20and%20Events/News/130422CDF_Millennials.aspx>.

40 Chris Welch, "Google Now will tell you if nearby stores have a product you've searched for," *The Verge,* 5 May 2014. Web. <http://www.theverge.com/2014/5/5/5684634/google-now-tracks-if-nearby-store-has-product-you-searched-for>.

41 Laura Petrecca, "Stores, Banks Go Speedy to Win Harried Customers," *USA Today,* 1 Dec. 2006. Web. <http://usatoday30.usatoday.com/money/perfi/general/2006-12-01-speedy-shopping-usat_x.htm?csp=34>.

42 Greg Bensinger, "Amazon Gets OK to Test Drones Outdoors," *The Wall Street Journal,* 15 Mar. 2015. Web. <http://www.wsj.com/articles/amazon-expands-one-hour-delivery-to-baltimore-miami-1426761703>.

43 The McCarthy Group, "Engaging Millennials," *The McCarthy Group,* Feb. 2014. Web. <http://themccarthygroup.com/what-we-do/millennials_survey/>.

44 Ad Age, "Target: Millennials," *Ad Age Cable Guide 2013,* n.d. Web. <http://brandedcontent.adage.com/cableguide2013/article.php?id=355>.

45 Ibid.

46 Jeff Fromm, "How to Get Millennials to Love and Share Your Product," *Advertising Age,* 14 Aug. 2013. Web. <http://adage.com/article/cmo-strategy/millennials-love-brand/243624/>.

47 "Observations from Capital Group Analysts Around the World," *Capital Group Quarterly Insights,* Winter 2014, 20.

48 Jon Quast, "3 Companies Cashing In on Online Ordering," *The Motley Fool,* 13 Jan. 2014. Web. <http://www.fool.com/investing/general/2014/01/13/3-companies-cashing-in-on-online-ordering.aspx>.

49 "Case Study: Jell-O Pudding Face Mood Meter," *We Are Social,* n.d. Web. <http://wearesocialau.tumblr.com/post/8377495518/case-study-jell-o-pudding-face-mood-meter-the>.

50 Robin Lewis, "Millennials: Double Trouble for Retail," *Forbes,* 30 Apr. 2014. Web. <http://www.forbes.com/sites/robinlewis/2014/04/30/millennials-double-trouble-for-retail/>.

51 Fromm, "How to Get Millennials to Love and Share Your Product" (see note 47).

52 "Millennials 2015 Favorite Brand Ranking Report," Moosylvania.com, n.d. Web report. <http://moosylvania.com/millennials/Moosylvania_Millennial_Study_2015.pdf>.

53 Elena Holodny, "Goldman Sachs and Teen Vogue: Here Are the 50 Brands that Young Women Love," *Business Insider,* 9 Oct. 2014. Web. <http://www.businessinsider.com/goldman-and-vogue-brands-for-millennials-2014-2014-10?op=1>.

54 Amy Gesenhues, "Survey: Millennials More Likely to Rank Tech Brands, But Google Still At Top of Everyone's List," *Marketing Land,* 5 Oct. 2013. Web. <http://marketingland.com/top-25-brands-survey-shows-tech-brands-favored-more-by-millennials-but-google-still-at-top-of-everyones-list-60794>.

Ann Arnof Fishman is president of Generational Targeted Marketing, LLC, a specialized marketing firm that provides insights into the preferences, trends, and buying habits of each of America's six generations. She was awarded four U.S. Senate Fellowships to study generational trends and taught generational marketing at New York University.

CPSIA information can be obtained at www.ICGtesting.com
Printed in the USA
BVOW02s0943010416

442588BV00001B/2/P